All *the* Best *for* Christmas

21
Choral Favorites
for Pageant, Concert,
or Worship Service

by

Camp Kirkland • Tom Fettke • Richard Kingsmore

Steven Curtis Chapman • Benjamin Harlan • Christopher Machen Joel

Lindsey • Dennis Allen • Lowell Alexander • Doug Holck

Bob Kauflin • Ken Bible • Dave Williamson • and more

Lillenas PUBLISHING COMPANY

www.lillenas.com

This Child Is the One

Words and Music by
DAVE and JAN WILLIAMSON
Arranged by Camp Kirkland,
Tom Fettke and Dave Williamson

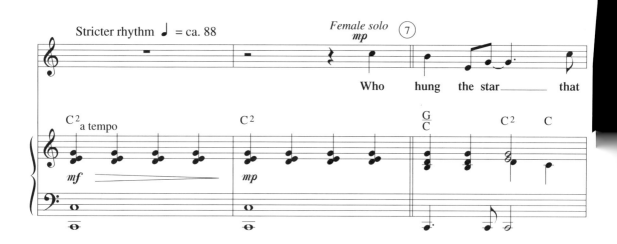

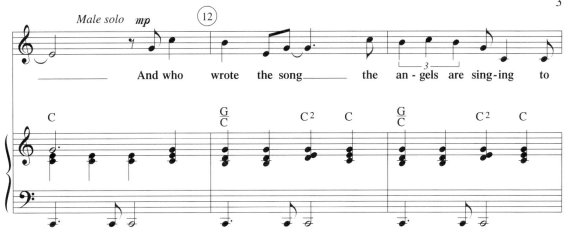

And who wrote the song_____ the an - gels are sing-ing to

wel - come this pre - cious sight?_____ Who

sche-duled this ho - ly mo - ment in time long be - fore time be-gan?_

6

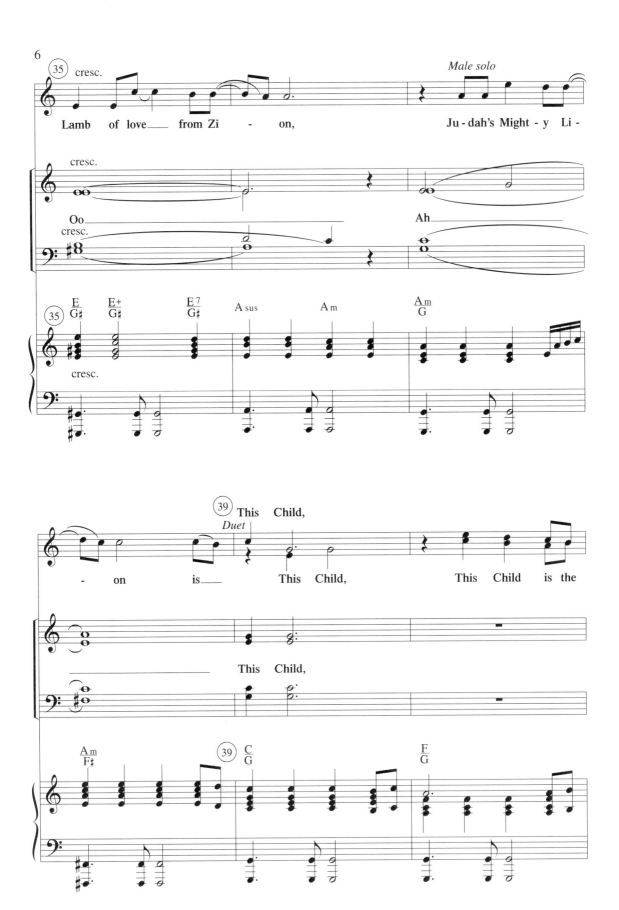

CD 1:3

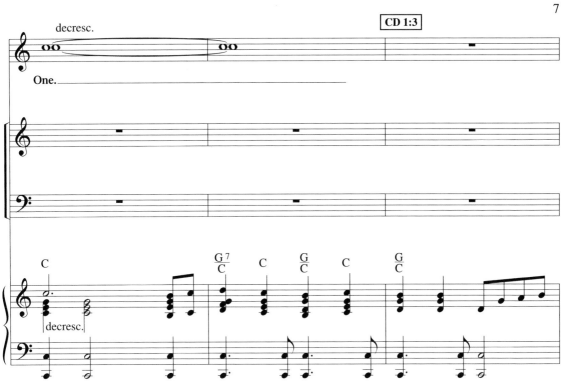

just the touch of His hand? And whose voice will si-lence the Voice will

si-lence,_____ Oo_____

an - gry sea with the pow - er His pres-ence com - mands?

9

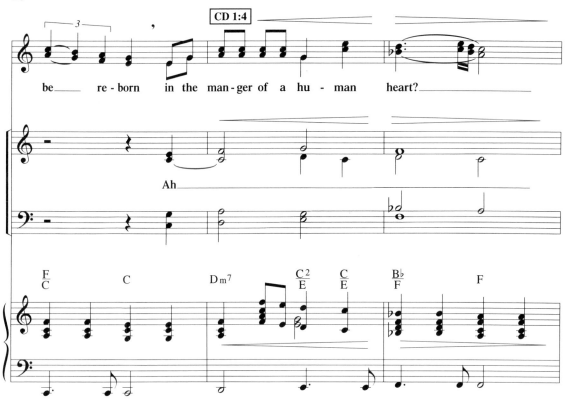

be____ re - born in the man - ger of a hu - man heart?____

Ah____

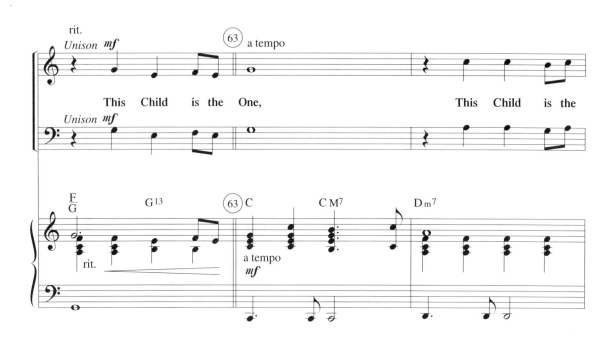

This Child is the One, This Child is the

12

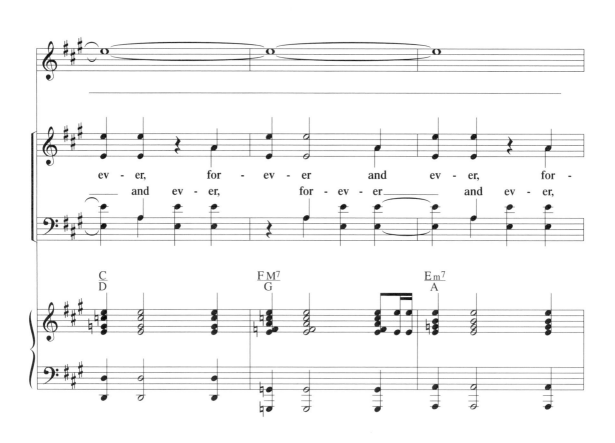

Jesus, O What a Wonderful Child

Traditional and
KEN BIBLE

African American Traditional
Arranged by Tom Fettke

Gospel shuffle ♩ = ca. 122

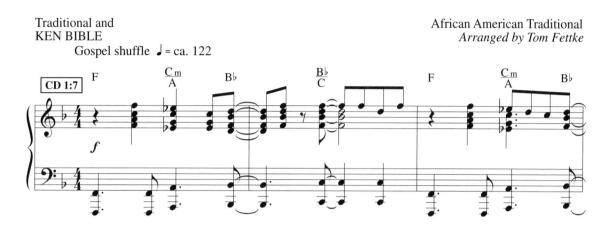

what a won-der-ful Child,_____

O_____ what a won-der-ful Child.

Je - sus,   Je - sus,   so low-ly_____

Je - sus,   Je - sus,   So low-ly,_____ meek and

24

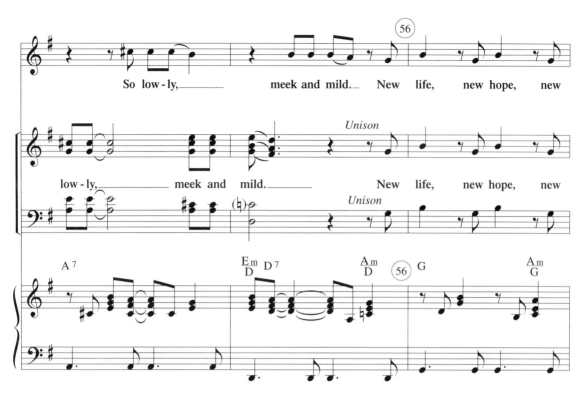

32

Heaven's Child

Words and Music by
JOEL LINDSEY
*Arranged by Camp Kirkland
and Tom Fettke*

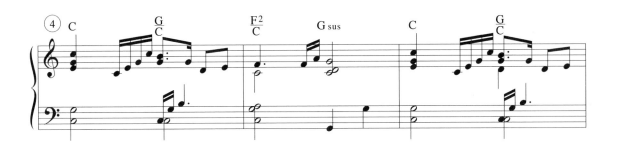

1. She rocked her ti - ny ba - by to___
(2. The) an - gels must___ have kissed Him as they

38

40

Child. Mar - y's lit - tle ba - by boy was

Ah

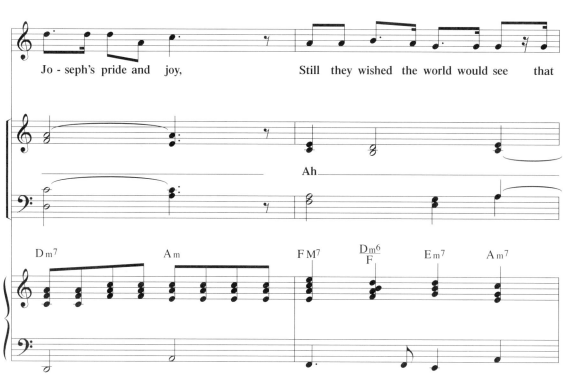

Jo - seph's pride and joy, Still they wished the world would see that

Ah

42

Canticle of Joy

Sing Joy
Joy to the World
How Great Our Joy!

Arranged by Camp Kirkland
and Tom Fettke

*"Sing Joy"
Brightly, with energy ♩ = ca. 120

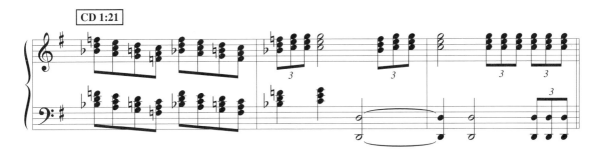

46

CD 1:24

Joy, joy, joy! Praise we the Lord in heav'n on high, on___ high. Joy to the world! the Sav-ior reigns; Let men their songs em-ploy While fields___ and___ floods,___ rocks,

52

Wise Men Still Seek Him

Words and Music by
CHRISTOPHER MACHEN
Arranged by Richard Kingsmore

Wise_____ men_____ still

seek_____ Him;_____ Thro' the shad-ow of night they

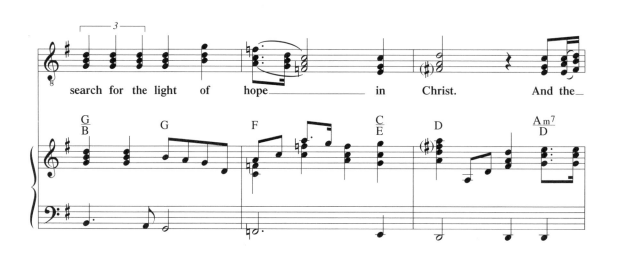

search for the light of hope_____ in Christ. And the__

62

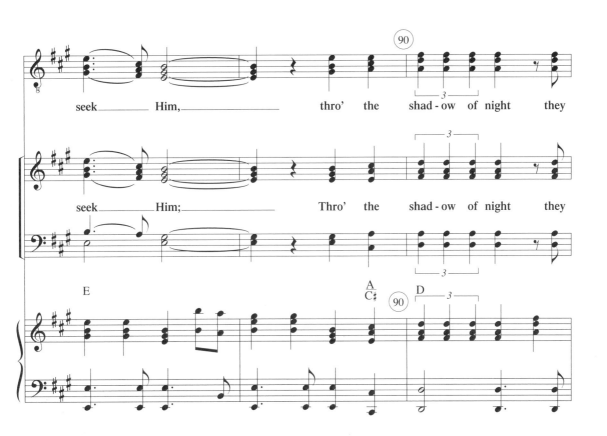

CD 1:31

search for the light of hope_____ in Christ. And the

search for the light of hope_____ in Christ. And the

dark - ness_____ gives way to the dawn_____

dark - ness_____ gives way to the dawn_____

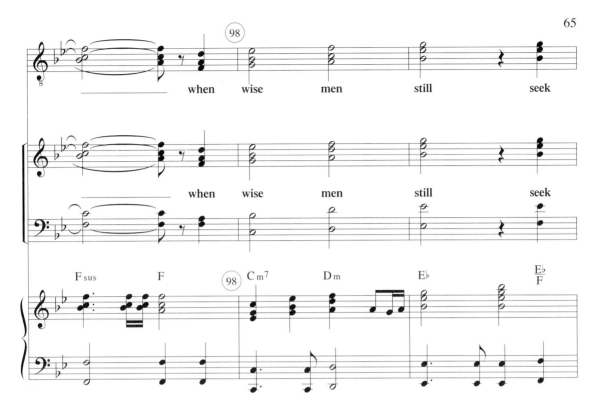

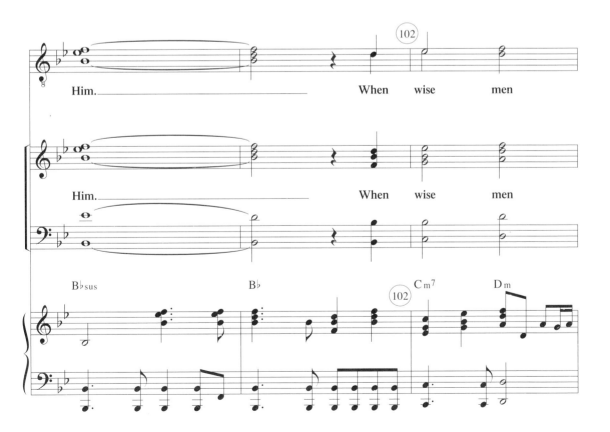

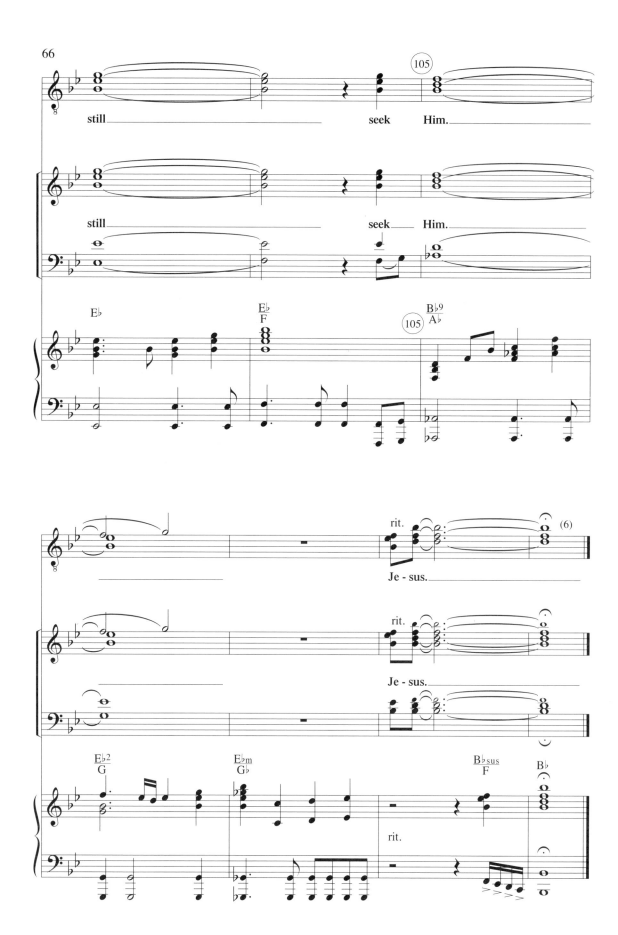

Jesus, the Light of the World

CHARLES WESLEY and
GEORGE D. ELDERKIN

GEORGE D. ELDERKIN
Arranged by Tom Fettke

70

72

76

Glory to God in the Highest

Words and Music by
DARYL WILLIAMS
Arranged by Camp Kirkland
and Tom Fettke

78

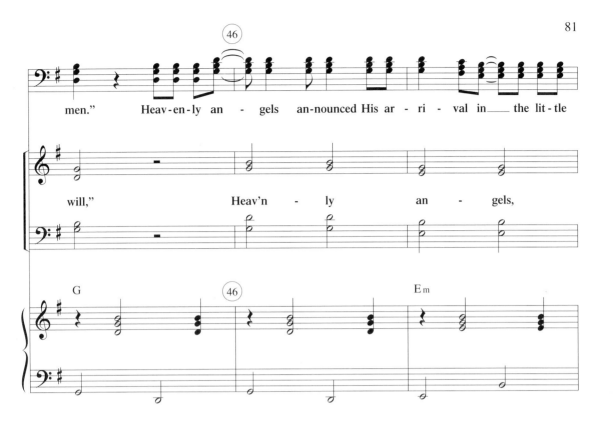

82

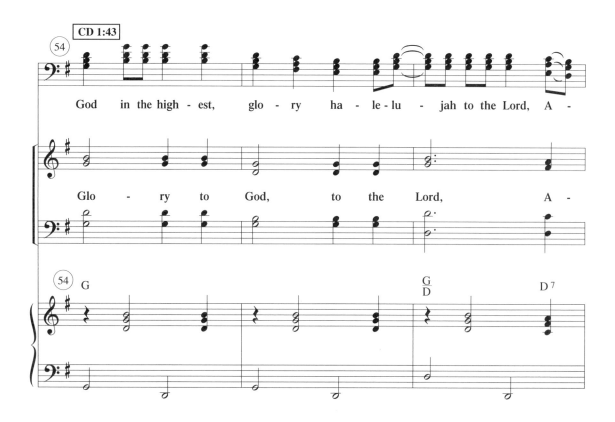

84

88

One Quiet Moment

Words and Music by
BOB KAUFLIN
Arranged by Dennis Allen

94

Adoration

Rev. JOHN S. B. MONSELL
and KEN BIBLE

TOM FETTKE

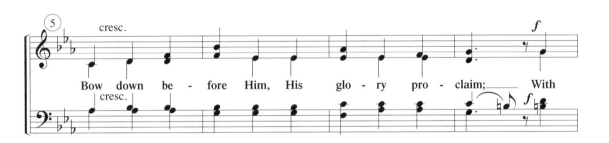

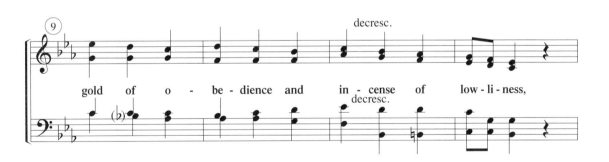

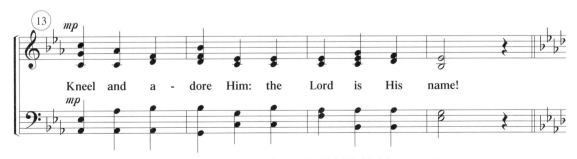

102

*For choirs having difficulty with full divisi, there is and optional SATB version of measures 25-28 at the end of the piece.

Child in the Manger

KEN BIBLE
and MARY MACDONALD

THOMAS J. WILLIAMS,
CAMP KIRKLAND and TOM FETTKE
Arranged by Camp Kirkland
and Tom Fettke

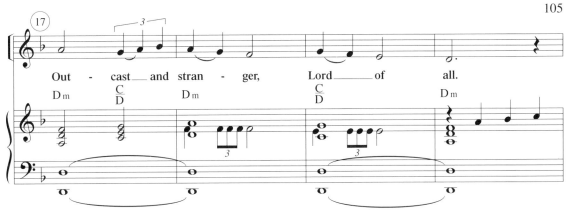

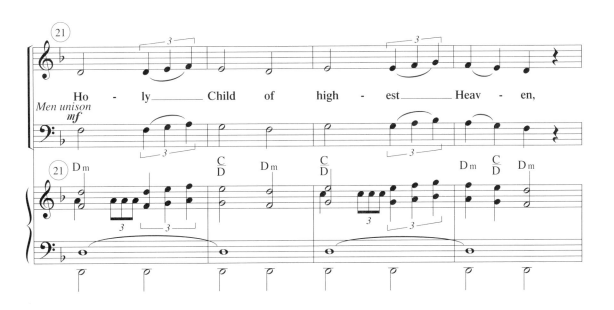

108

112

We Have Seen His Star

Words and Music by
BILL BATSTONE
Arranged by Doug Holck

PLEASE NOTE: Copying of this product is not covered by CCLI licenses. For CCLI information call 1-800-234-2446.

117

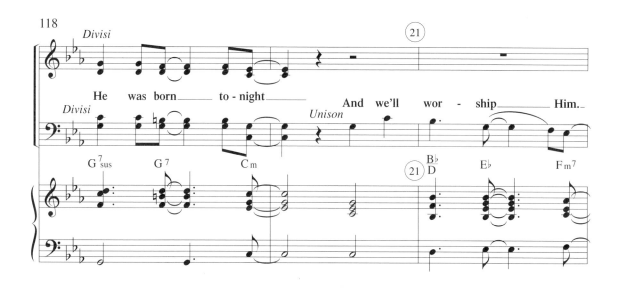

122

We have seen___ His star,_____ we have seen___ the Light!_

And we'll wor - ship___ Him.___ We'll

We'll wor - ship Him this

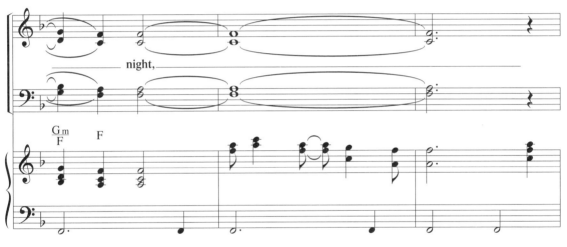

night,

this night.

126

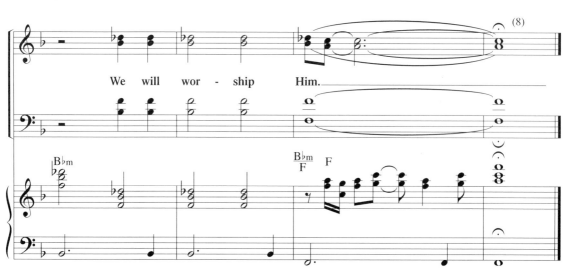

Amen

TOM FETTKE, KEN BIBLE
and Traditional

Traditional
Arranged by Richard Kingsmore

Joyfully, swing feel ♩ = ca. 114

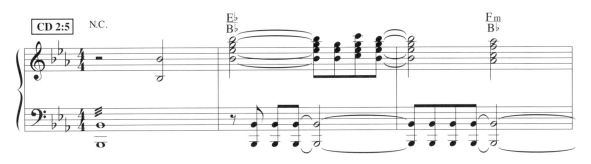

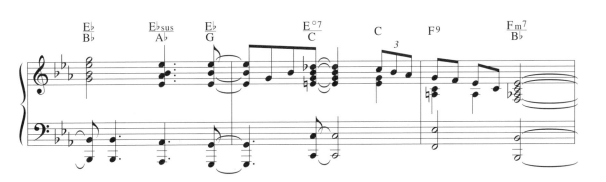

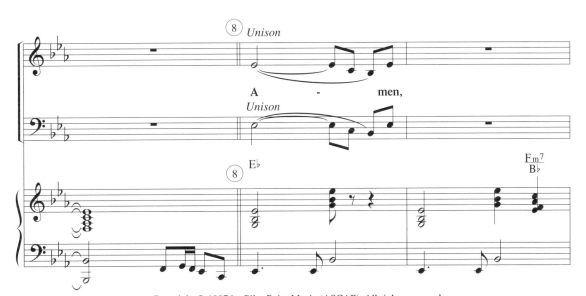

A - men,

128

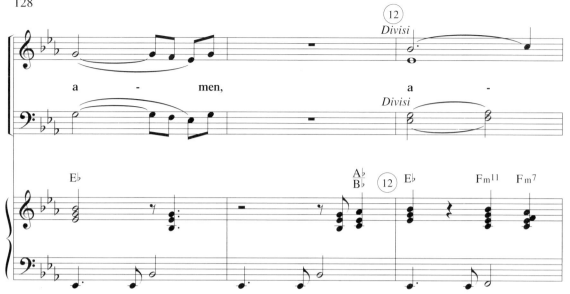

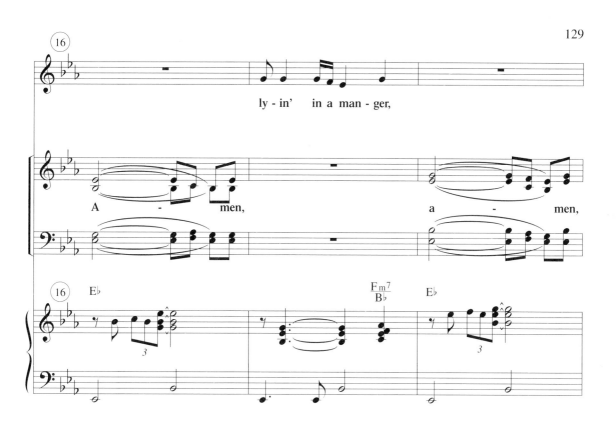

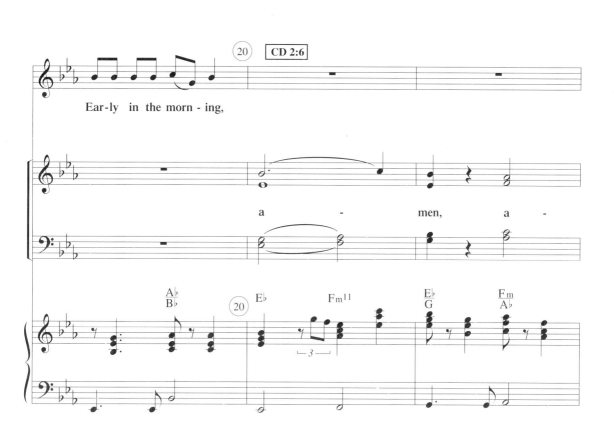

131

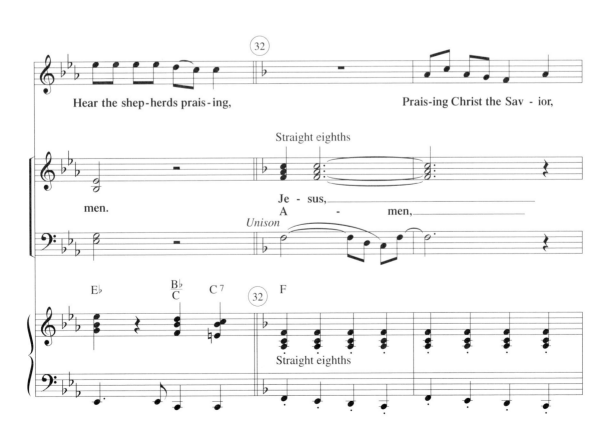

Shout-ing and re-joic - ing!

Je - sus, Je - sus, a -

a - men, A

Divisi

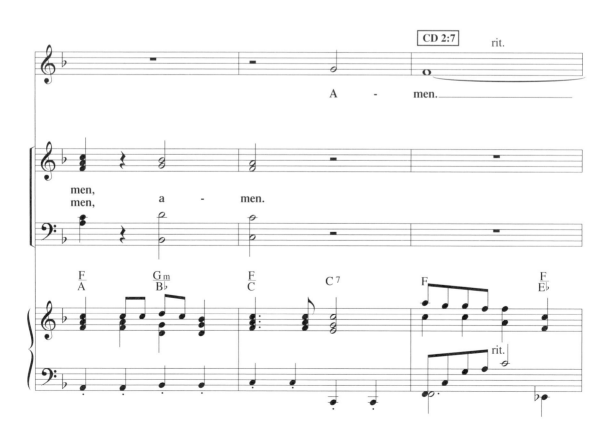

men,
men, a - men.

A - men.

CD 2:7   rit.

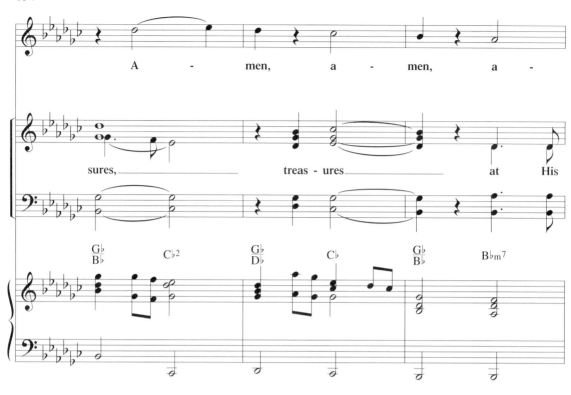

A - men, a - men, a -

sures,_____ treas - ures_____ at His

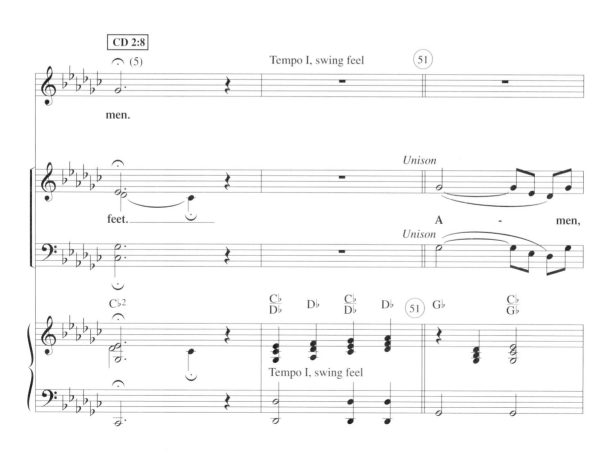

CD 2:8

(5)   Tempo I, swing feel   51

men.

feet._____

Unison

A -   men,

Unison

Tempo I, swing feel

Glo - ry hal - le - lu - jah,   Glo - ry in the high - est!___

a - men,

a - men,

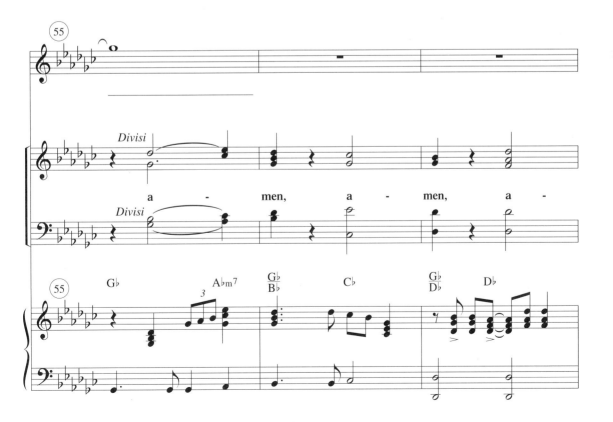

a - men,   a - men,   a -

138

Rose of Bethlehem

Words and Music by
LOWELL ALEXANDER
Arranged by Richard Kingsmore

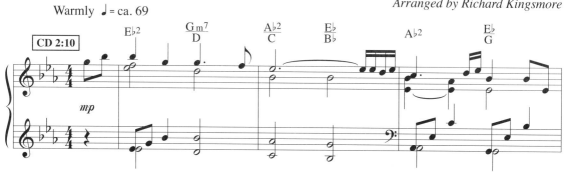

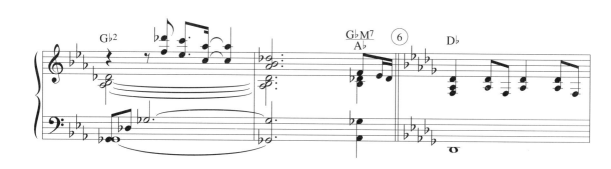

There's a Rose in Beth - le - hem, with a

PLEASE NOTE: Copying of this product is not covered by CCLI licenses. For CCLI information call 1-800-234-2446.

144

148

Beautiful Star of Bethlehem

ADGER M. PACE

R. FISCHER BOYCE
Arranged by Tom Fettke

154

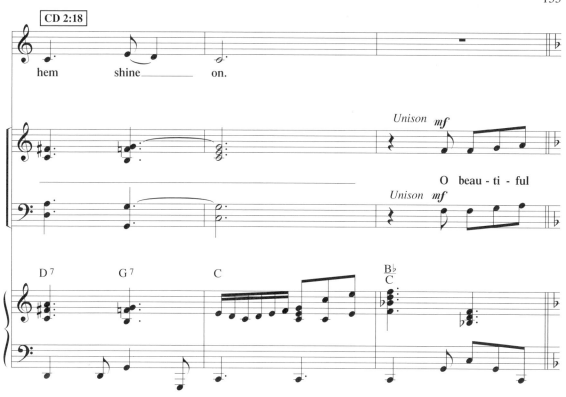

CD 2:20

161

O Come, O Come, Emmanuel

Latin Hymn;
Tr. by JOHN M. NEALE

STEVEN CURTIS CHAPMAN
Arranged by Tom Fettke

PLEASE NOTE: Copying of this product is not covered by CCLI licenses. For CCLI information call 1-800-234-2446.

come to thee, O Is - ra - el, re - joice!

CD 2:23

168

Sing We All Noel!

Sing We Now of Christmas
The First Noel

Arranged by Richard Kingsmore

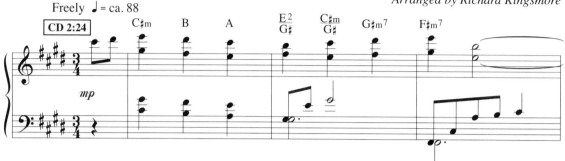

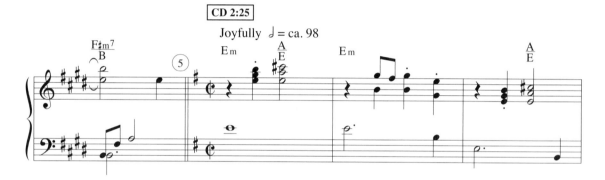

OPTIONAL CALL TO WORSHIP: Begin intro at measure 103, page 179; vocals begin at measure 106, using alternate lyrics.

172

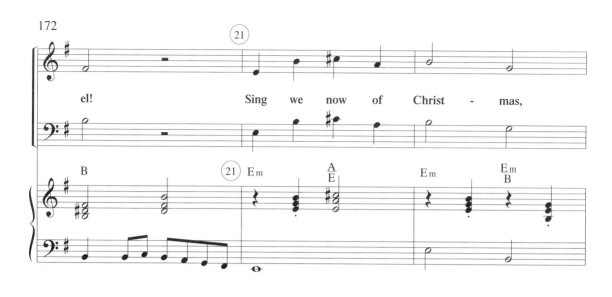

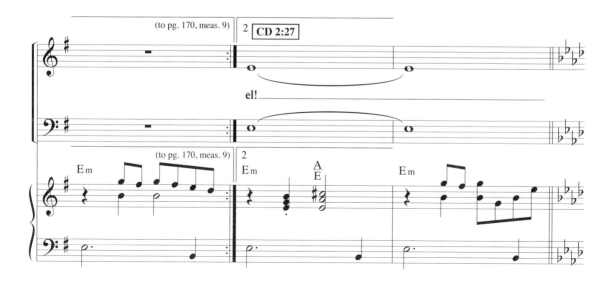

174

176 *"The First Noel"

*For optional Call to Worship, begin introduction at measure 103, CD point 2:30; vocals begin at measure 106, using alternate lyrics.

Who Is This Child?

PATRICIA KING STOWELL

BENJAMIN HARLAN
Arranged by Tom Fettke

184

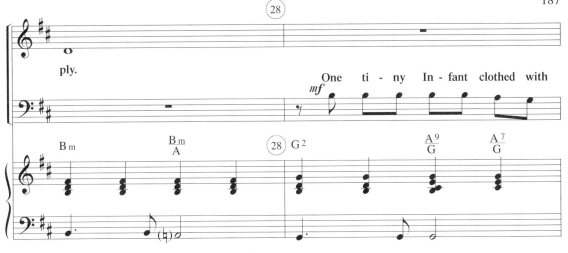

ply.

One ti - ny In - fant clothed with

grace,

Gives life to all who seek His face.

Who is this Child so sweet and mild?

Our Eyes Have Seen the Lord

LINDA LEE JOHNSON

TOM FETTKE

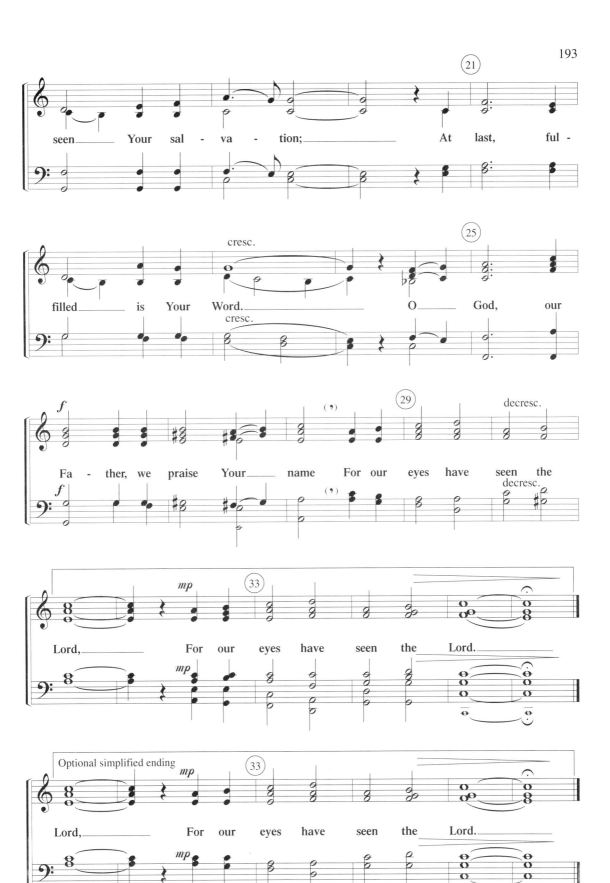

The Virgin Mary Had a Baby Boy

Traditional and
TOM FETTKE

Traditional
Arranged by Camp Kirkland
and Tom Fettke

1st time: Men unison
2nd time: All

1st time 8va through ms. 14

The vir - gin Mar - y had a ba - by boy,_____ The vir - gin Mar - y had a ba - by boy,_____ The vir - gin Mar - y had a

ba - by boy,_____ And they said that His name was Je -

Divisi

2nd time divisi

CD 2:36 1st time
CD 2:37 2nd time

sus, Je - sus. The

Unison

sus. And un - to us a bless-ed child is born,_____ And

Unison *mf*

A
mf

mf

199

A Cradle in the Shadow of a Cross

Words and Music by
DOROTHY L. SMITH
Arranged by Richard Kingsmore

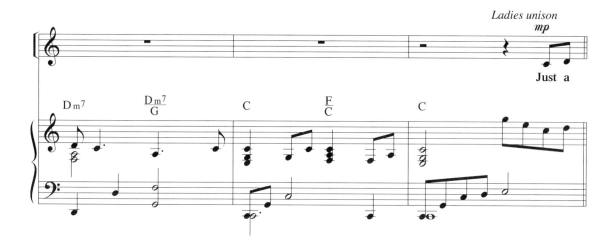

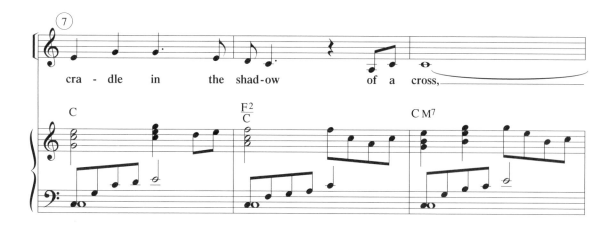

204

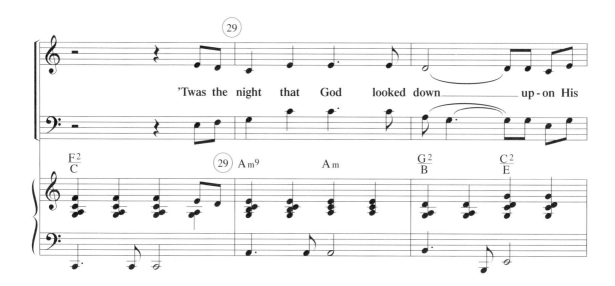

Angels Keep Rejoicing

with

Angels We Have Heard On High

Words and Music by
DOUG HOLCK
Arranged by Doug Holck

With excitement, swing feel ♩ = ca. 94

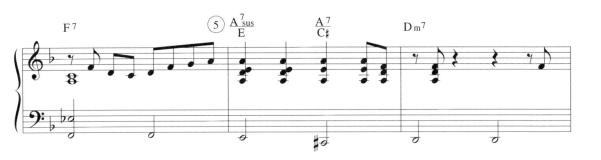

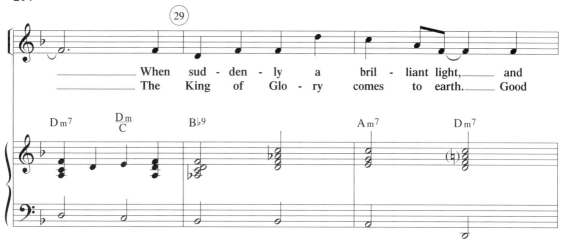

When sud - den - ly a bril - liant light,_____ and
The King of Glo - ry comes to earth.____ Good

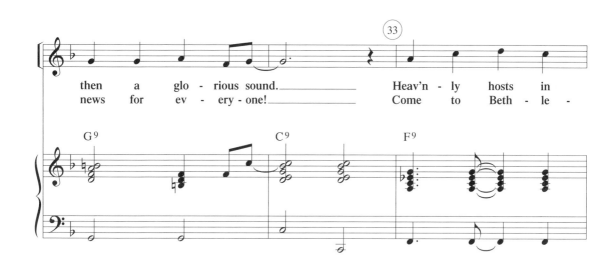

then a glo - rious sound._____ Heav'n - ly hosts in
news for ev - ery - one!_____ Come to Beth - le -

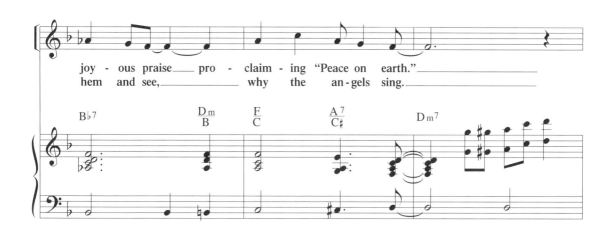

joy - ous praise___ pro - claim - ing "Peace on earth."_____
hem and see,_____ why the an - gels sing._____

Angels Keep Rejoicing

with

Angels We Have Heard On High

Words and Music by
DOUG HOLCK
Arranged by Doug Holck

With excitement, swing feel ♩ = ca. 94

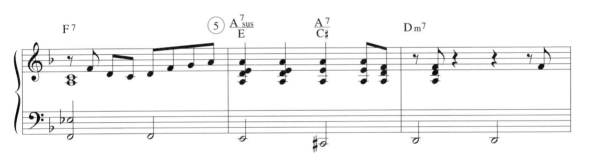

Glo - ri - a!

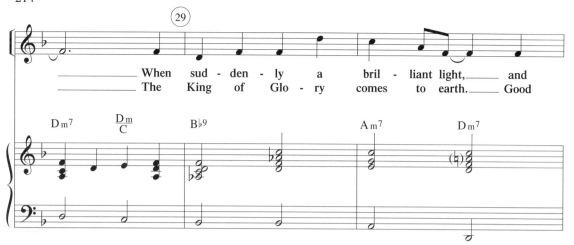

When sud - den - ly a bril - liant light,_____ and
The King of Glo - ry comes to earth._____ Good

Dm7   Dm/C   B♭9   Am7   Dm7

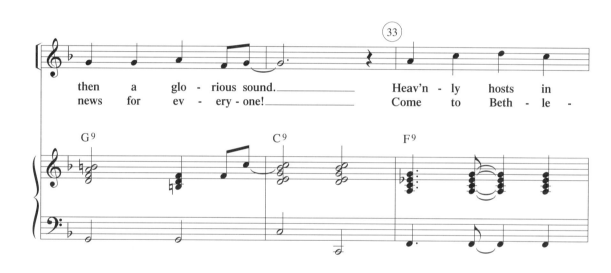

then a glo - rious sound._____ Heav'n - ly hosts in
news for ev - ery - one!_____ Come to Beth - le -

G9   C9   F9

joy - ous praise_____ pro - claim - ing "Peace on earth."_____
hem and see,_____ why the an - gels sing._____

B♭7   Dm/B   F/C   A7/C♯   Dm7

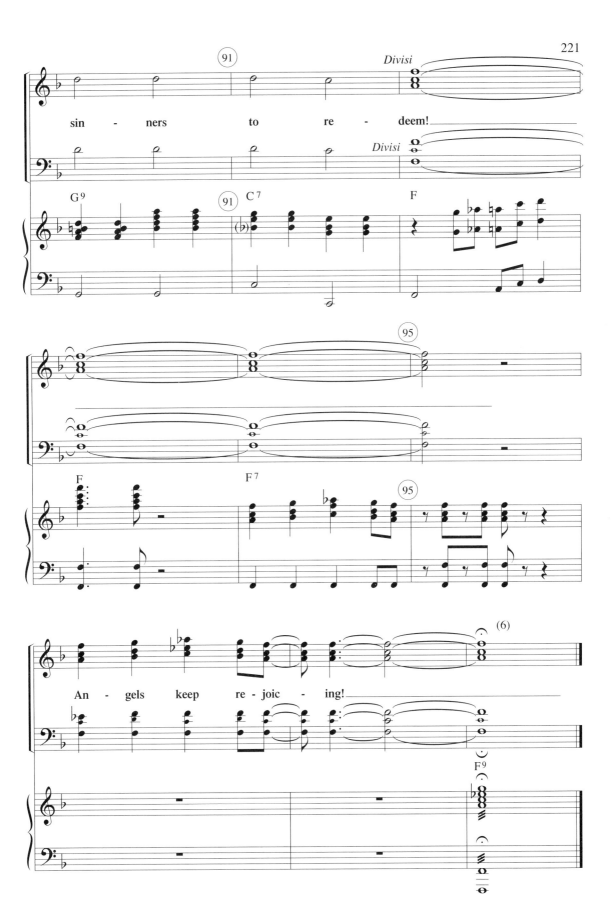

sin - ners to re - deem!

An - gels keep re - joic - ing!

TOPICAL INDEX

Angels & Shepherds

Amen 127
Angels Keep Rejoicing *with* Angels
   We Have Heard on High . . . 211
Child in the Manger 104
Glory to God in the Highest . . . 77
Jesus, the Light of the World . . . 67
SING WE ALL NOEL! 170
Who Is This Child? 183

At the Manger

A Cradle in the Shadow of
   a Cross 202
Amen 127
Child in the Manger 104
Heaven's Child 36
Our Eyes Have Seen the Lord . . 192

Atonement

A Cradle in the Shadow of
   a Cross 202
Child in the Manger 104
Jesus, the Light of the World . . . 67
Rose of Bethlehem 140
The Virgin Mary Had a
   Baby Boy 194

His Life & Ministry

This Child Is the One 2

Life Application

Wise Men Still Seek Him 55

Light

Jesus, the Light of the World . . . 67

Mary & Joseph

Heaven's Child 36
One Quiet Moment 92

Old Testament Prophecy

O Come, O Come, Emmanuel . . 162
SING WE ALL NOEL! 170
The Virgin Mary Had a
   Baby Boy 194

Praise & Worship

Adoration 101
Amen 127
CANTICLE OF JOY 45
Heaven's Child 36
Jesus, O What a Wonderful
   Child 21
Our Eyes Have Seen the Lord . . 192
SING WE ALL NOEL! 170
This Child Is the One 2
Who Is This Child? 183

Simeon

Our Eyes Have Seen the Lord . . 192

Wise Men & the Star

Adoration 101
Amen 127
Beautiful Star of Bethlehem . . 149
SING WE ALL NOEL! 170
We Have Seen His Star 116
Who Is This Child? 183
Wise Men Still Seek Him 55

ALPHABETICAL INDEX

A Cradle in the Shadow of a Cross 202

Adoration 101

Amen 127

Angels Keep Rejoicing *with* Angels
  We Have Heard on High 211

Beautiful Star of Bethlehem 149

CANTICLE OF JOY 45

  Sing Joy

  Joy to the World

  How Great Our Joy!

Child in the Manger 104

Glory to God in the Highest 77

Heaven's Child 36

Jesus, O What a Wonderful Child 21

Jesus, The Light of the World 67

O Come, O Come, Emmanuel 162

One Quiet Moment 92

Our Eyes Have Seen the Lord 192

Rose of Bethlehem 140

SING WE ALL NOEL! 170

  Sing We Now of Christmas

  The First Noel

The Virgin Mary Had a Baby Boy 194

This Child Is the One 2

We Have Seen His Star 116

Who Is This Child? 183

Wise Men Still Seek Him 55